mi casa

an introduction to commonly used Spanish words and phrases around the home, with 500 lively photographs

JEANINE BECK

southwater

Contents

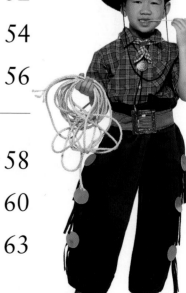

Learning Spanish

Introduce your child to Spanish from an early age by combining everyday words and phrases with lively photographs of daily activities in and around the home. Your child will enjoy learning Spanish. Let them look at the pictures and read and remember the Spanish words and phrases that accompany them. Encourage them to say the words aloud.

 ## A NEW LANGUAGE

There is a growing need today for everyone to speak a second language. All children should have the chance to access a new language. Research shows children aged 2–8 are most receptive to linguistic learning. The younger the child, the easier it is to learn. The Spanish used in Latin America and the United States differs from that spoken in Spain, in pronunciation and vocabulary. The most noticeable difference in American pronunciation is the 's' sound as in "cena" (seh-na) or "zapato" (sa-pat-oh). This is pronounced in Spain as 'th' – "theh-na", " tha-pat-oh".

 ## PRACTICING TOGETHER

Children can enjoy practicing their Spanish all around your home. Encourage them to look at the furniture, toys and objects in each room and say the Spanish words aloud. They can use their new Spanish vocabulary to talk to their pets and when they are playing with their friends or helping you in the kitchen. You may have some Spanish-speaking friends who can talk to your children. All this will give your children a brilliant head start when they begin formal Spanish lessons at school.

LEARNING WITH PICTURES

Children respond very well to photographs and will enjoy finding pictures of things they know. Help them say and learn the Spanish words for these pictures of pets, toys and household objects around them. They can use Spanish to count things or to tell you the colors of their clothes. They will find out the names of all the rooms in their home. Let them take you round the house and use Spanish words to describe the things you can see.

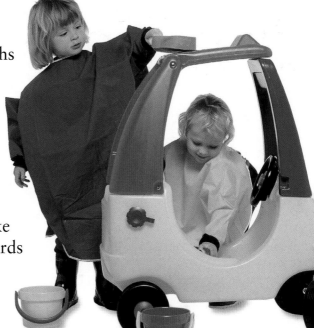

IT'S FUN TO LEARN

Make learning fun by using the vocabulary on an everyday basis. Children need to demonstrate what they have learnt by playing games. You could play 'I-Spy' by choosing an object you can see and then making the sound that the word begins with or saying what color it is. Ask your child to guess what Spanish word you are thinking of and say the word aloud. The book covers such important themes as colors, counting, opposites, food and much more. Bright and informative photographs will help the children build up their knowledge of commonly used Spanish words and phrases in a fun way. This will give them the confidence to speak Spanish.

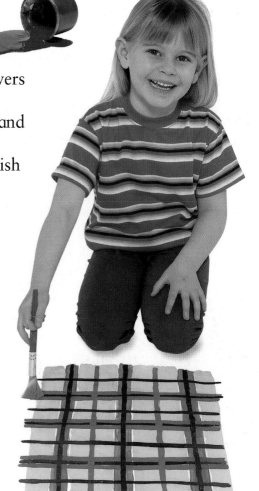

HOW THE BOOK IS STRUCTURED

The key words on each page are highlighted and translated in vocabulary panels. Sentences on each page appear in both Spanish and English to help your child understand. At the end of every section is a question-and-answer game with a puzzle for you to do together and give the child a real sense of achievement. The dictionary lists all the key words and explains how they should be pronounced. Reward certificates at the end of the book test your child's knowledge of Spanish and develop confidence and self-esteem.

Mi casa

My home is special. Your home is special, too. Look at the pictures and say the words in Spanish aloud. Then use your Spanish to take your friends and family on a guided tour of your home.

La cocina

The kitchen is a fun place to work. Everyone can help to get meals ready and then tidy up.

Nos gusta preparar tortas.
We like making cakes.

el rodillo

los huevos

el bol

la tortera

Say it with me

| el colador | la tortera | los huevos | el rodillo |
| sieve | cake tin | eggs | rolling pin |

¡Qué sucio! ¿Quién lo limpiará?
What a mess! Who will clean it up?

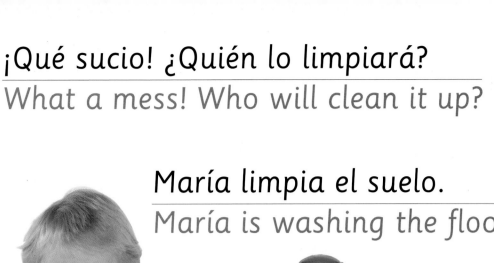

María limpia el suelo.
María is washing the floor.

David

el detergente

María

el trapeador

el repasador

David seca los platos.
David dries the plates.

la cubeta

el bol	el repasador	el detergente	el trapeador	la cubeta
bowl	dishtowel	detergent	mop	bucket

El salón

The sitting room is a family room. You can read or play games or talk or watch television.

Quiero leer.

I want to read.

el gatito

la bola

el cojín muy grande

Pero nosotros ¡queremos jugar!

But we want to play!

Say it with me

los libros	el cojín muy grande	la bola	el gatito
books	big cushion	ball	kitten

Luís monta un rompecabezas.
Luís is doing a jigsaw puzzle.

Luís

Alicia construye un castillo.
Alicia is building a castle.

Alicia

los cubos

el rompecabezas

¿De qué color son los cubos?
What colors are the bricks?

el rompecabezas	**el cubo amarillo**	**el cubo verde**	**el cubo rojo**	**el cubo azul**
jigsaw	yellow brick	green brick	red brick	blue brick

El comedor

The dining room is a room where everyone can sit and talk over a meal.

Pedro pone la mesa.

Pedro is laying the table.

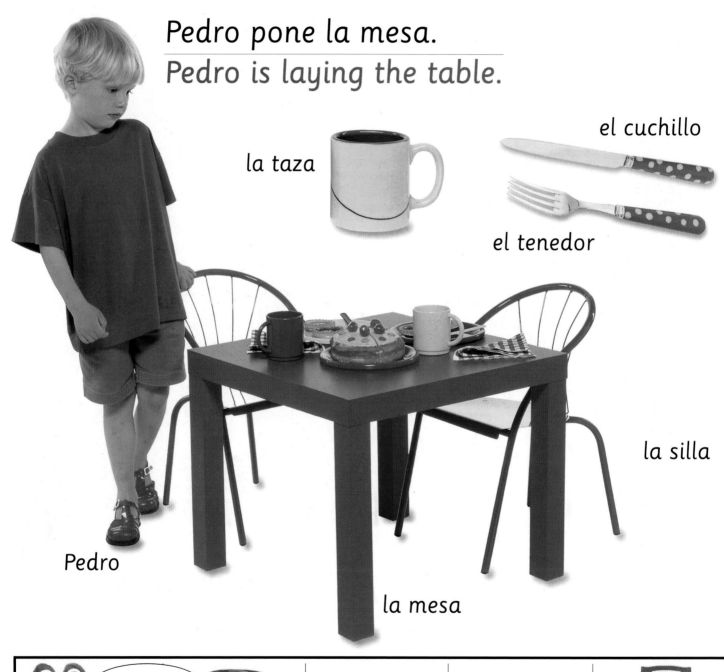

la taza

el cuchillo

el tenedor

la silla

Pedro

la mesa

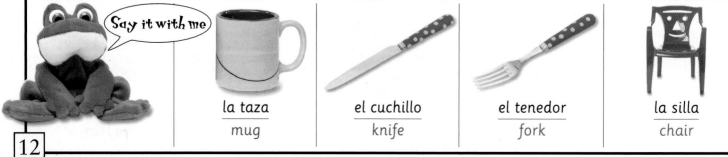

Say it with me

la taza	el cuchillo	el tenedor	la silla
mug	knife	fork	chair

12

Llevo los vasos.
I'll bring the glasses.

el plato

la pizza

dos vasos

la charola

Nos gusta comer la cena.
We like eating dinner.

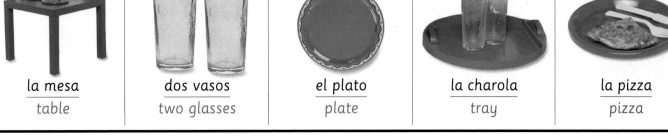

la mesa	dos vasos	el plato	la charola	la pizza
table	two glasses	plate	tray	pizza

13

El cuarto de juegos

The play room is a special place to play in. Some children keep their toys and paints in a big toy box.

¿Qué pintas, Daniel?
What are you painting, Daniel?

Sandra

los lápices de colores

el dibujo

el cuadro

Daniel

la caja de pinturas

Pinto nuestra casa, Sandra.
I'm painting our house, Sandra.

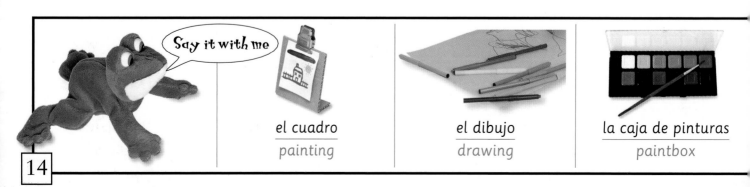

Say it with me

el cuadro
painting

el dibujo
drawing

la caja de pinturas
paintbox

¿Te gusta bailar?
Do you like dancing?

las notas musicales

la casetera

Me gusta escuchar música.
I like listening to music.

las herramientas

Puedo reparar las cosas.
I can mend things.

los lápices de colores
pencils

la casetera
cassette player

las herramientas
tools

las notas musicales
music notes

El dormitorio

The bedroom is the place to keep your clothes and all your favorite books and toys.

¿Quieres un cuento, Osito?
Do you want a story, Teddy?

los libros

el osito

Sí, por favor.
Yes, please.

Say it with me

los libros	el osito	la biblioteca
books	teddy bear	bookcase

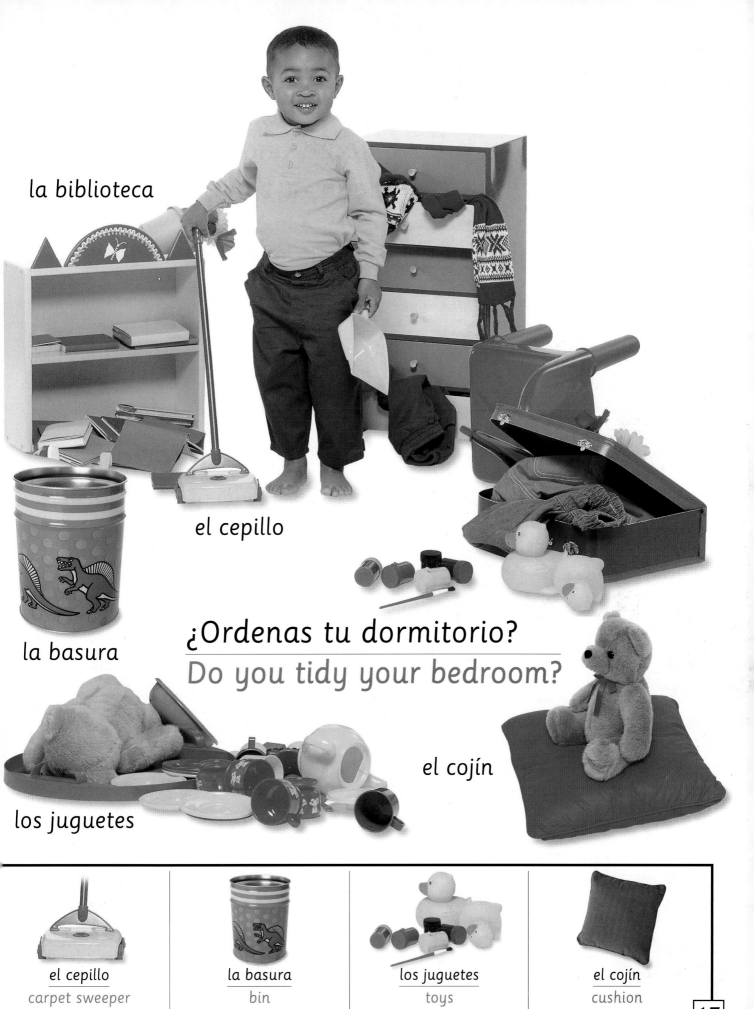

la biblioteca

el cepillo

la basura

los juguetes

¿Ordenas tu dormitorio?
Do you tidy your bedroom?

el cojín

el cepillo	la basura	los juguetes	el cojín
carpet sweeper	bin	toys	cushion

El baño

The bathroom is full of steam and soap and hot water. A bath gets you clean at the end of the day.

¿Quieres tomar un baño?
Would you like a bath?

el jabón líquido

el jabón

No, gracias.
No, thank you.

la bañera latina

la toalla

la esponja

Say it with me

el jabón	el jabón líquido	la esponja	la bañera latina
soap	bubble bath	sponge	bathtub

Me cepillo los dientes.
I am brushing my teeth.

Yo también.
Me too.

el dentífrico

el cepillo
de dientes

el pato

el barquito

¿Cuántos patos hay?
How many ducks are there?

el barquito	la toalla	el cepillo de dientes	el dentífrico	el pato
boat	towel	toothbrush	toothpaste	duck

El jardín

The garden is really hot today! Let's go out to plant flowers, play ball and paddle.

Estamos en el jardín.
We are in the garden.

las flores

la regadera

la jardinera

¿Cuántas niñas hay?
How many girls are there?

Say it with me

la jardinera	las flores	la regadera
plant pot	flowers	watering can

¿Quién atrapará la bola?
Who will catch the ball?

la niña pequeña

el niño

la niña grande

la alberca inflable

¡El agua está fría!
The water is cold!

la niña grande	la niña pequeña	el niño	la alberca inflable
big girl	little girl	boy	paddling pool

El garaje

The garage is the place to keep cars and bikes and scooters. Sonia keeps her bike in the garage.

Sonia tiene un triciclo.
Sonia has a tricycle.

el osito

el triciclo

Sonia

¡Sujétate bien, Osito!
Hold on, Teddy!

el monopatín

Say it with me

el monopatín	el osito	el triciclo	el carro
scooter	teddy bear	tricycle	car

Lavamos el carro.
We are washing the car.

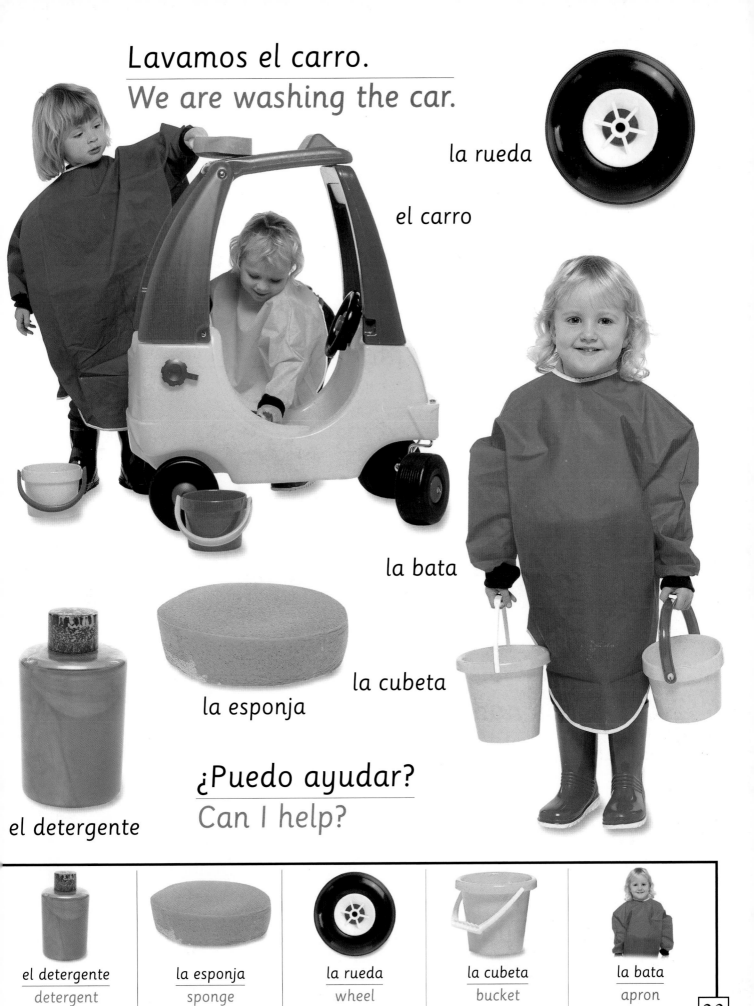

la rueda

el carro

la bata

la cubeta

la esponja

el detergente

¿Puedo ayudar?
Can I help?

el detergente	la esponja	la rueda	la cubeta	la bata
detergent	sponge	wheel	bucket	apron

Puzzle time

Now you know about the rooms in your home. Write the missing words in the sentences and fill in the crossword with the words in Spanish.

1 Las flores crecen en el jardín.

The flowers are growing in the _ _ _ _ _ _ _ .

2 Los patos nadan en el baño.

The ducks swim in the _ _ _ _ _ .

3 Guardo mi triciclo en el garaje.

I keep my tricycle in the _ _ _ _ _ _ _ .

4 Leo un libro en el salón.

I am reading in the _____ _____.

5 Comemos la cena en el comedor.

We are eating _____ in the dining room.

Now try my crossword!

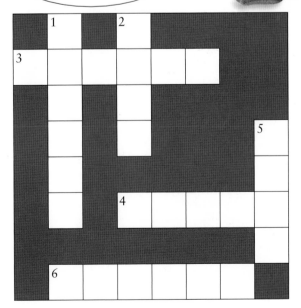

	1		2		
3					

6 Limpio el suelo de la cocina.

I am washing the _____ floor.

25

Un día
en casa

A day at home gives you a chance to talk to your family and pets in Spanish. Look at these colorful photographs of the things you do every day – and say the words aloud. You can speak Spanish.

Levantarse

Getting up in the morning is easy for some people. Other people need an alarm clock.

Buenos días, Osito.
Good morning, Teddy.

Miranda

el reloj

Buenos días, Miranda.
Good morning, Miranda.

la cama

la manta

los zapatos

| Say it with me | la cama bed | la manta blanket | el reloj clock | los pantalones pants |

¡Mira! Estoy vestida.
Look! I'm dressed.

la camisa

la pollera

los pantalones

el enterito

las medias

Me pongo el suéter.
I am putting on my sweater.

los zapatos shoes	**la camisa** shirt	**la pollera** skirt	**las medias** socks	**el enterito** dungarees

29

Desayunar

Eating breakfast is a good way to start the morning. What do you want to eat today?

¿Qué hay para desayunar?
What's for breakfast?

las tostadas

el huevo frito

el bolillo

la manteca

 Say it with me

la manteca	el bolillo	el huevo frito	las tostadas
butter	bread roll	fried egg	toast

la leche

el jugo de manzana

la miel

Como los cereales.
I am eating cereal.

la fruta

los cereales

la miel	la leche	el jugo de manzana	la fruta	los cereales
honey	milk	apple juice	fruit	cereal

Jugar con mis amigos

Playing with friends is fun! They can visit you
at home, and you can play lots of games.

Ven a nuestra merienda.
Come to our tea party.

la tetera

¿Puedes contar las tazas?
Can you count the cups?

los ositos

Say it with me

la cuchara	el plato	la tetera	la taza
spoon	plate	teapot	cup

¿Dónde está todo el mundo?

Where is everyone?

la valija

Estoy en la valija.

I am in the suitcase.

la caja de sorpresas

la
ventana

Estoy en la caja.

I am in the box.

la casa

la puerta

Estamos en la casa.

We are in the house.

la valija suitcase	**la ventana** window	**la casa** house	**la puerta** door	**la caja de sorpresas** jack in the box

Un paseo en el parque

A walk in the park gets you out of the house.
You can walk the dog and feed the ducks.

¿Vamos al parque?
Shall we go to the park?

Magdalena

el perro

la ardilla

el pato

Sí, por favor, Magdalena.
Yes, please, Magdalena.

la correa

Say it with me

el perro
dog

la correa
leash

la ardilla
squirrel

Queremos dar de comer a los patos.
We want to feed the ducks.

la bolsa

las botas

Doy de comer a los patos.
I am feeding the ducks.

el patito

---

la bolsa	las botas	el pato	el patito
bag	boots	duck	duckling

La hora de cenar

Dinnertime is the main meal of the day.
What do you like eating best?

¿Qué vamos a cenar hoy?
What shall we eat today?

la pasta

las papas fritas

la leche

Say it with me

la pasta
pasta

la leche
milk

las papas fritas
French fries

la fruta
fruit

la fruta

el pollo

el queso

la salchicha

el queso

las galletitas de perro

las verduras

Victor tiene hambre.
Victor is hungry.

el pollo	el queso	la salchicha	las verduras	las galletitas de perro
chicken	cheese	sausage	vegetables	dog biscuits

La hora de dormir

Bedtime is sleepy time. You can read a book in bed or listen to a story or just go to sleep.

¡No tengo sueño!
I'm not sleepy!

la cama

el perro

el dragón

¿Cuántos animales hay en la cama?
How many animals are in the bed?

¡Buenas noches!
Good night!

el gato

Say it with me

el dragón	la cama	el perro
dragon	bed	dog

¿Qué te pones para dormir?
What do you wear at bedtime?

la bata

la piyama

¿Dónde están mis pantuflas?
Where are my slippers?

las pantuflas

el gato
cat

la piyama
pajamas

la bata
dressing gown

las pantuflas
slippers

Puzzle time

Some words are missing from the sentences.
Can you fill them in and complete the Lost
Letters puzzle with their Spanish names?

Me gustan los cereales.
I like _ _ _ _ _ _ _ .

El reloj marca la hora.
The _ _ _ _ _ _ tells the time.

Al osito le gusta la casa.
The _ _ _ _ _ _ _ _ _ _ likes the _ _ _ _ _ _ .

La niña come un hot dog y papas fritas.
The ____ eats a hot dog and _____.

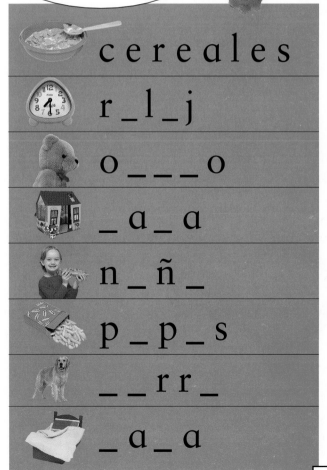

El perro es marrón.
The ___ is brown.

Try to find the lost letters

El dragón se va a la cama.
The dragon goes to ___.

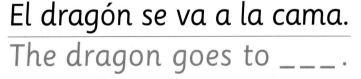

c e r e a l e s

r _ l _ j

o _ _ _ o

_ a _ a

n _ ñ _

p _ p _ s

_ _ r r _

_ a _ a

La hora de jugar

Playtime is the happiest part of the day, and you can practice your Spanish at the same time! You can speak Spanish while you are playing games or having fun with your friends.

Pintar

Painting is a messy thing to do! You can paint with a paintbrush or your hands or feet.

Mis pantalones tienen cuadros.
My pants have checks.

los pinceles

la caja
de pinturas

Me gusta pintar cuadros.
I like painting checks.

Say it with me

los pinceles
brushes

la caja de pinturas
paintbox

negro
black

blanco
white

44

¿Te gusta mi cuadro?
Do you like my painting?

azul

negro

amarillo

rojo

blanco

verde

¡Pinto con mis pies!
I'm painting with my feet!

naranja

rojo	amarillo	azul	naranja	verde
red	yellow	blue	orange	green

Tocar música

Making music is great fun. Some people play instruments, others like to dance.

la araña

¿Bailas?
Are you dancing?

el gatito

la bailarina

No. Estoy cazando una araña
No. I'm catching a spider.

Say it with me

la bailarina	el gatito	la araña	la guitarra
dancer	kitten	spider	guitar

Toco la guitarra.
I play the guitar.

la flauta

el tambor

la guitarra

la pandereta

el xilófono

la trompeta

¿Sabes tocar el xilófono?
Can you play the xylophone?

el tambor
drum

la flauta
recorder

la pandereta
tambourine

la trompeta
trumpet

el xilófono
xylophone

Disfrazarse

Dressing up is an adventure. You can be a pretty fairy or a magic wizard.

Tengo una varita mágica.
I have a wand.

el mago

la varita mágica

el sombrero

el hada

Soy un mago.
I'm a wizard.

Say it with me

el hada	la varita mágica	el sombrero	el mago
fairy	wand	hat	wizard

¿Puedes ver mi loro?
Can you see my parrot?

el vaquero

el payaso

el pirata

el loro

¿Dónde está mi placa?
Where's my badge?

Soy un payaso.
I'm a clown.

la placa

el pirata
pirate

el loro
parrot

el payaso
clown

el vaquero
cowboy

la placa
badge

49

De compras

Playing shops is fun. Count the food before you put it in your shopping basket.

¿Qué voy a comprar?
What shall I buy?

una barra de pan

dos tortas

tres helados

la canasta

cuatro bananas

Say it with me

la canasta
basket

una barra de pan
one bread loaf

dos tortas
two cakes

tres helados
three ice creams

cuatro bananas
four bananas

cinco bombones

seis manzanas

siete galletitas

ocho cerezas

nueve tomates

diez latas

Estoy de compras.

I am shopping.

inco bombones	seis manzanas	siete galletitas	ocho cerezas	nueve tomates	diez latas
five chocolates	six apples	seven cookies	eight cherries	nine tomatoes	ten cans

Bajo la lluvia

Getting wet is fantastic fun.
You can splash in all the puddles.

la lluvia

Me caí en la charca.
I fell in the puddle.

las botas

la charca

Me gusta jugar en la lluvia
I like playing in the rain.

Say it with me

la charca	las botas	la lluvia
puddle	boots	rain

Nos gusta pescar bajo la lluvia.
We like fishing in the rain.

la capucha

la caña de pescar

el pez

el impermeable

¡Hemos capturado dos peces!
We've caught two fish!

el impermeable	la capucha	la caña de pescar	el pez
raincoat	rainhat	fishing rod	fish

Los juegos

la bola

Playing games is fun. You can play with your friends and get some exercise too!

¿Puedes lanzar una bola?

Can you throw a ball?

el casco

lanzar

la bicicleta

¿Quién gana la carrera?

Who is winning the race?

Say it with me

la bola
ball

lanzar
throw

el casco
helmet

la bicicleta
bike

Nos gusta practicar deporte.
We like sport.

los patines

el monopatín

el fútbol

¿Quién está arriba?
Who is high?

los bolos

saltar

¿Quién está abajo?
Who is low?

el fútbol
football

los patines
roller skates

el monopatín
skateboard

los bolos
skittles

saltar
jump

Puzzle time

Can you count from one to six? Here are some clues. The Spanish numbers are in the Word Square

Un niño lanza una bola.

___ boy is throwing a ball.

Dos niños pescan.

___ boys are fishing.

Tres instrumentos musicales.

_____ musical instruments.

Cuatro niños saltan.
_ _ _ _ children are jumping.

El payaso hace
malabarismos con cinco bolas.
The clown is juggling _ _ _ _ balls.

Find the Spanish
numbers in my
word square

Seis huellas.
_ _ _ footprints.

a	c	u	a	t	r	o
u	h	a	b	r	l	o
n	o	t	c	e	a	q
o	u	r	c	s	n	q
o	n	c	i	n	c	o
d	o	s	x	a	n	o
c	h	i	s	e	i	s

How Spanish works

Encourage your child to enjoy learning Spanish and go further in the language. You may find these basic tips on how the Spanish language works helpful. Check out the dictionary, since it lists all the key words in the book and will help you and your child pronounce the words correctly.

MASCULINE/FEMININE

All nouns are masculine (el, un) or feminine (la, una). 'Los' or 'unos' are used in the plural for masculine nouns, 'las' or 'unas' for feminine nouns.

COMPARING THINGS

When we want to compare things in English, we say they are, for example, small, smaller or smallest. This is the pattern in Spanish:

SPANISH	ENGLISH
Es pequeño	He is small
Es más pequeño	He is smaller
Es el más pequeño	He is the smallest

ADJECTIVES

As a general rule, feminine adjectives end in 'a' (e.g. la niña pequeña) and masculine adjectives in 'o' (e.g. el niño pequeño). If the adjective does not end in 'o' or 'a' it does not change.

PERSONAL PRONOUNS

SPANISH	ENGLISH
yo	I
tú	you (singular)
usted	you (singular polite)
él or ella	he or she
nosotros	we
ustedes	you (plural)
ellos or ellas	they

'Tú' is used for talking to people you know and 'usted' is used when talking to someone you don't know and are being polite. 'Ustedes' is used when you are talking to more than one person.

Verbs

Spanish verbs change their endings depending on which personal pronoun and tense are used. This book uses only the present tense but there are other tenses in Spanish including the past and the future.

Help your child find the language pattern that emerges in the endings of the Spanish verbs. There are three groups of verbs which follow a regular pattern: those that end in 'ar', 'er' and 'ir'. Point out that in the verbs given here, 'tú' either ends in '-as' or '-es' and 'usted' either in '-a' or '-e' whilst 'ustedes' ends in '-an' or '-en'. Play a game by saying the first word aloud – 'Yo', 'Tú'. Let your child answer with the verb – 'salto', 'saltas'.

Here are three simple verbs in the present tense. Look at the ends of the words and say the Spanish out loud.

SPANISH	ENGLISH
saltar	**to jump**
Yo salto	I jump
Tú saltas	You jump
Usted salta	You jump (polite)
Él/ella salta	He/she jumps
Nosotros saltamos	We jump
Ustedes saltan	You jump (plural)
Ellos/ellas saltan	They jump

SPANISH	ENGLISH
comer	**to eat**
Yo como	I eat
Tú comes	You eat
Usted come	You eat (polite)
Él/ella come	He/she eats
Nosotros comemos	We eat
Ustedes comen	You eat (plural)
Ellos/ellas comen	They eat

SPANISH	ENGLISH
decir	**to say**
Yo digo	I say
Tú dices	You say
Usted dice	You say (polite)
Él/ella dice	He/she says
Nosotros decimos	We say
Ustedes dicen	You say (pl.)
Ellos/ellas dicen	They say

Pronunciation Key

SPANISH	SAY	EXAMPLE
a	a	cama: ka-ma
ai	eye	bailarina: bye-la-ree-na
e	eh	leche: leh-cheh
u	oo	lunes: loo-nez
ue	weh	puerta: pwehr-ta
b	b	bolsa: bol-sa
v	b	vaso: ba-soh
c	k	casa: ka-sa
c	s	cepillo: seh-pee-yoh
h	this is not pronounced	hada: ada
g	g	gato: ga-toh
g	h	mágica: ma-hika
j	h	jabón: ha-bon
gu	g	juguetes: hoo-geh-tez
ll	jsh	ardilla: ar-dee-jsha
ñ	ny	bañera: ban-yehr-a
z	s	taza: ta-sa

El diccionario

ENGLISH	SPANISH	SAY

A

apple	la manzana	*la man-san-a*
apple juice	el jugo de manzana	*el hoo-goh deh man-san-a*
apron	la bata	*la ba-ta*

B

badge	la placa	*la pla-ka*
bag	la bolsa	*la bol-sa*
ball	la bola	*la boh-la*
banana	la banana	*la ba-na-na*
basket	la canasta	*la kan-asta*
bathroom	el baño	*el ban-yoh*
bathtub	la bañera latina	*la ban-yehr-a lat-ee-na*
bed	la cama	*la ka-ma*
bedroom	el dormitorio	*el dor-mee-tor-ee-oh*
bike	la bicicleta	*la bee-see-kleh-ta*
bin	la basura	*la bas-oo-ra*
boat	el barquito	*el bar-keet-oh*
bookcase	la biblioteca	*la bib-lee-oh-teh-ka*
books	los libros	*los lee-broz*
boots	las botas	*las boh-taz*
bowl	el bol	*el bol*
boy	el niño	*el nee-nyo*

Colors

ENGLISH	SPANISH	SAY
black	negro	*neh-groh*
blue	azul	*a-sool*
brown	marrón	*mar-ron*
green	verde	*behr-deh*
gray	gris	*grees*
orange	naranja	*na-ran-ha*
red	rojo	*roh-hoh*
white	blanco	*blan-koh*
yellow	amarillo	*am-ar-ee-jshoh*

60

ENGLISH	SPANISH	SAY
bread loaf	la barra de pan	*la bar-ra deh pan*
bread roll	el bolillo	*el bol-ee-jshoh*
breakfast	el desayuno	*el des-a-yoo-noh*
brick	el cubo	*el koo-boh*
brushes	los pinceles	*los pin-seh-lez*
bubble bath	el jabón líquido	*el hab-on lee-ki-doh*
bucket	la cubeta	*la koo-beh-ta*
butter	la manteca	*la man-teh-ka*

C

cake	la torta	*la tor-ta*
cake pan	la tortera	*la tor-tehr-a*
can	la lata	*la la-ta*
car	el carro	*el kar-roh*
carpet sweeper	el cepillo	*el seh-pee-jshoh*
cassette player	la casetera	*la kas-et-ehra*
cat	el gato	*el ga-toh*
cereal	los cereales	*los seh-reh-al-ez*
chair	la silla	*la see-jsha*
cheese	el queso	*el keh-soh*
cherries	las cerezas	*las seh-reh-saz*
chicken	el pollo	*el po-jshoh*
chocolates	los bombones	*los bom-boh-nez*
clock	el reloj	*el reh-loh*
clown	el payaso	*el pa-ya-soh*
cookies	las galletitas	*las ga-jshet-eet-az*
cowboy	el vaquero	*el bak-ehr-oh*
cup	la taza	*la ta-sa*
cushion	el cojín	*el ko-heen*

D

dancer	la bailarina	*la bye-la-ree-na*
detergent	el detergente	*el deh-tehr-hen-teh*
dining room	el comedor	*el ko-meh-dohr*
dinner	la cena	*la seh-na*
dishtowel	el repasador	*el re-pas-a-dor*
dog	el perro	*el per-roh*
dog biscuits	las galletitas de perro	*las ga-jshet-eet-az deh per-roh*
door	la puerta	*la pwehr-ta*
dragon	el dragón	*el dra-gon*
drawing	el dibujo	*el dee-boo-hoh*

Days of the week

ENGLISH	SPANISH	SAY
Monday	lunes	*loo-nez*
Tuesday	martes	*mar-tez*
Wednesday	miércoles	*mee-ehr-koh-lez*
Thursday	jueves	*hweh-bez*
Friday	viernes	*bee-ehr-nez*
Saturday	sábado	*sa-ba-doh*
Sunday	domingo	*do-ming-goh*

ENGLISH	SPANISH	SAY
dressing gown	la bata	*la ba-ta*
drum	el tambor	*el tam-bohr*
duck	el pato	*el pa-toh*
duckling	el patito	*el pa-tee-toh*
dungarees	el enterito	*el en-tehr-eet-oh*

E

eggs	los huevos	*los weh-boz*

F

fairy	el hada	*el ada*
fish	el pez	*el pes*
fishing rod	la caña de pescar	*la kan-ya deh pes-kar*
flowerpot	la maceta	*la ma-seh-ta*
football	el fútbol	*el foot-bol*
fork	el tenedor	*el teh-neh-dohr*
French fries	las papas fritas	*las pa-pas free-tas*
fried egg	el huevo frito	*el weh-boh free-toh*
fruit	la fruta	*la froo-ta*

G

garage	el garaje	*el gar-a-heh*
garden	el jardín	*el har-deen*
girl	la niña	*la nee-nya*
glass	el vaso	*el ba-soh*
guitar	la guitarra	*la gee-tar-ra*

ENGLISH	SPANISH	SAY

H

helmet	el casco	*el kas-koh*
honey	la miel	*la mee-yel*
house	la casa	*la ka-sa*

I and J

ice cream	el helado	*el eh-la-doh*
jack in the box	la caja de sorpresas	*la ka-ha deh sor-preh-saz*
jigsaw	el rompecabezas	*el rom-peh-ka-beh-saz*

K

kitchen	la cocina	*la koh-see-na*
kitten	el gatito	*el ga-tee-toh*
knife	el cuchillo	*el koo-chee-jshoh*

L and M

leash	la correa	*la kor-reh-a*
mechanical	mecánico	*meh-kan-i-koh*
milk	la leche	*la leh-cheh*
mop	el trapeador	*el trap-eh-a-dor*

Months of the year

ENGLISH	SPANISH	SAY
January	enero	*en-ehr-oh*
February	febrero	*feb-rehr-oh*
March	marzo	*mar-soh*
April	abril	*ab-reel*
May	mayo	*ma-yoh*
June	junio	*hoo-nee-oh*
July	julio	*hoo-lee-oh*
August	agosto	*ag-ost-oh*
September	septiembre	*sep-tee-em-breh*
October	octubre	*ok-too-breh*
November	noviembre	*nob-ee-em-breh*
December	diciembre	*dis-ee-em-breh*

ENGLISH	SPANISH	SAY
mug	la taza	*la ta-sa*
music notes	las notas musicales	*las noh-taz moo-zik-al-ez*

P

ENGLISH	SPANISH	SAY
paddling pool	la alberca inflable	*la al-behr-ka in-fla-bleh*
paintbox	la caja de pinturas	*la ka-ha deh peen-too-raz*
painting	el cuadro	*el kwad-roh*
pajamas	la piyama	*la pee-yama*
pants	los pantalones	*los pan-tal-ohn-ez*
parrot	el loro	*el lo-roh*
pasta	la pasta	*la pas-ta*
pencils	los lápices	*los lap-i-sez*
pirate	el pirata	*el pee-ra-ta*
pizza	la pizza	*la peet-za*
plant pot	la jardinera	*la har-dee-nehr-a*
plate	el plato	*el pla-toh*
play room	el cuarto de juegos	*el kwar-toh deh hweh-goz*
puddle	la charca	*la char-ka*

R

ENGLISH	SPANISH	SAY
rain	la lluvia	*la jshoo-bee-a*
raincoat	el impermeable	*el im-pehr-meh-ableh*
rainhat	la capucha	*la ka-poo-cha*
recorder	la flauta	*la flaoo-ta*
roller skates	los patines	*los pa-tee-nez*

Numbers

ENGLISH	SPANISH	SAY
one	uno (m.)/una (f.)	*oo-no/oo-na*
two	dos	*dos*
three	tres	*tres*
four	cuatro	*kwa-troh*
five	cinco	*sing-koh*
six	seis	*seh-ees*
seven	siete	*see-eh-teh*
eight	ocho	*och-oh*
nine	nueve	*noo-eh-beh*
ten	diez	*dee-es*

ENGLISH	SPANISH	SAY

S

ENGLISH	SPANISH	SAY
sausage	la salchicha	*la sal-chee-cha*
scooter	el monopatín	*el mono-pa-teen*
shirt	la camisa	*la ka-mee-sa*
shoes	los zapatos	*los sa-pa-toz*
sieve	el colador	*el kol-a-dor*
sitting room	el salón	*el sal-on*
skateboard	el monopatín	*el mono-pa-teen*
skirt	la pollera	*la po-jsheh-ra*
skittles	los bolos	*los boh-loz*
slippers	las pantuflas	*las pan-too-flaz*
soap	el jabón	*el ha-bon*
socks	las medias	*las meh-dee-az*
soft toy	el muñeco de peluche	*el moo-nyeh-koh deh pel-oo-cheh*
spider	la araña	*la ar-anya*
sponge	la esponja	*la es-pong-ha*
spoon	la cuchara	*la koo-chara*
squirrel	la ardilla	*la ar-dee-jsha*
suitcase	la valija	*la bal-ee-ha*
sun	el sol	*el sol*

T

ENGLISH	SPANISH	SAY
table	la mesa	*la meh-sa*
tambourine	la pandereta	*la pan-deh-reh-ta*
teapot	la tetera	*la teh-teh-ra*
teddy bear	el osito	*el os-ee-toh*
to jump	saltar	*sal-tar*
to throw	lanzar	*lan-sar*
toast	la tostada	*la tos-ta-da*
tools	las herramientas	*las err-a-mee-en-taz*
toothbrush	el cepillo de dientes	*el seh-pee-jshoh deh dee-en-tez*
toothpaste	el dentífrico	*el den-ti-free-koh*
towel	la toalla	*la toh-a-jsha*
toys	los juguetes	*los hoo-geh-tez*
tray	la charola	*la cha-roh-la*
trumpet	la trompeta	*la trom-peh-ta*

V, W and X

ENGLISH	SPANISH	SAY
vegetables	las verduras	*las behr-doo-raz*
wand	la varita mágica	*la bar-ee-ta ma-hika*
watering can	la regadera	*la reh-ga-dehr-a*
wheel	la rueda	*la rweh-da*
window	la ventana	*la ben-ta-na*
wizard	el mago	*el ma-goh*
xylophone	el xilófono	*el zee-lof-on-oh*

This is to certify that

_____

can count
from one to ten
in Spanish

Date _____

This is to certify that

_____

can name
six colors
in Spanish

Date _____

This is to certify that

_____

can name
five toys
in Spanish

Date _____

This is to certify that

_____

can name the
rooms in a house
in Spanish

Date _____

This edition is published by Southwater, an imprint of Anness Publishing Ltd, Hermes House, 88–89 Blackfriars Road, London SE1 8HA; tel. 020 7401 2077; fax 020 7633 9499 www.southwaterbooks.com; www.annesspublishing.com

If you like the images in this book and would like to investigate using them forpublishing, promotions or advertising, please visit our website www.practicalpictures.com for more information.

UK agent: The Manning Partnership Ltd;
tel. 01225 478444; fax 01225 478440; sales@manning-partnership.co.uk
UK distributor: Grantham Book Services Ltd;
tel. 01476 541080; fax 01476 541061; orders@gbs.tbs-ltd.co.uk
North American agent/distributor: National Book Network;
tel. 301 459 3366; fax 301 429 5746; www.nbnbooks.com
Australian agent/distributor: Pan Macmillan Australia;
tel. 1300 135 113; fax 1300 135 103; customer.service@macmillan.com.au
New Zealand agent/distributor: David Bateman Ltd;
tel. (09) 415 7664; fax (09) 415 8892

Publisher: Joanna Lorenz
Managing Editor: Linda Fraser
Editor: Joy Wotton
Designer: Maggi Howells
Photography: Jane Burton, John Daniels, John Freeman, Robert Pickett, Kim Taylor, Lucy Tizard

ETHICAL TRADING POLICY

At Anness Publishing we believe that business should be conducted in an ethical and ecologically sustainable way, with respect for the environment and a proper regard to the replacement of the natural resources we employ.

As a publisher, we use a lot of wood pulp to make high-quality paper for printing, and that wood commonly comes from spruce trees. We are therefore currently growing more than 750,000 trees in three Scottish forest plantations: Berrymoss (130 hectares/320 acres), West Touxhill (125 hectares/305 acres) and Deveron Forest (75 hectares/185 acres). The forests we manage contain more than 3.5 times the number of trees employed each year in making paper for the books we manufacture.

Because of this ongoing ecological investment programme, you, as our customer, can have the pleasure and reassurance of knowing that a tree is being cultivated on your behalf to naturally replace the materials used to make the book you are holding.

Our forestry programme is run in accordance with the UK Woodland Assurance Scheme (UKWAS) and will be certified by the internationally recognized Forest Stewardship Council (FSC). The FSC is a non-government organization dedicated to promoting responsible management of the world's forests. Certification ensures forests are managed in an environmentally sustainable and socially responsible way. For further information about this scheme, go to www.annesspublishing.com/trees

A CIP catalogue record for this book is available from the British Library.

The publishers wish to thank all the children who appear in this book.

Y ahora,
¡tú sabes
hablar español!